A Year Without the Grocery Store
Companion Workbook

Dedication

Steve, these last six months have brought changes to our family. <u>A Year Without the Grocery Store</u> was published. We moved into a new home and started this new business. We even graduated a daughter from high school. You are my rock in the midst of all the craziness. I love you so much, and I'm so thankful for you.

ACKNOWLEDGEMENTS

To my kids, Ian, Jordan, Shannen, Ethan, and Nathan. I am so proud of each of you, how you are growing both in body, in knowledge, and in spirit.

Ally, your consistent encouragement throughout this last year has now resulted in two published works. Thank you for keeping me at it when things were hard. Keep up the work on your own books! You amaze me with what you are capable of and how much you have accomplished.

Niki, thank you for your friendship. You bring such joy and encouragement to my life. You are as true a friend as they come!

Author Biography

On Good Friday in 2011, our house in Ferguson, Missouri was hit by an F4 tornado. Many people write about food storage from their accumulating of food storage during easy times. They have a knowledge of it, but haven't had to really live it.

I haven't written about food storage because of our abundance, but because we've had to live from our food storage out of necessity. We lived through that F-4 tornado that hit our house. While the tornado didn't completely destroy our home, we were displaced by it. Having food storage in our house allowed me to literally pack up three week's worth of food and take it to the hotel in which the insurance company was putting us up. I didn't have to think about food or menus or about money to eat out every meal. This knowledge gave me the freedom to focus on getting things settled with the insurance company. I had the freedom to keep my kids going and to deal with them not feeling safe. I had the freedom to run to different places to sign documents or make the different phone calls to deal with the devastation the storm wreaked on our home.

Since that time, I've lived through two other life-changing events. I was an eye-witness to the Ferguson riots. No matter which side of the equation you come down on, it was life-changing and eye opening. I also lived through an armed standoff with a knife wielding man during my family's time at a local homeschool chess club. This taught me the importance of knowing how to react before something happens, so you get it right. You don't have time to think things over. Each of these things taught me a new level of self-sufficiency and preparedness.
I never knew what life was going to throw at me, but my journey to self-sufficiency started with food storage and grew beyond my wildest imaginings.

If you are interested in finding out more about me, Karen Morris, or A Year Without the Grocery Store, you can visit me here: http://ayearwithoutthegrocerystore.com.

Preparedness is kind of like blogging. It's a long journey with a steep learning curve! The whole purpose of this *Companion Workbook to A Year Without the Grocery* Store is to help level out that learning curve.

- Walks you through setting up your long-term food storage.
- Takes you step by step through how to decide on your short-term food storage menu.
- Takes your menu and helps you break down each meal's ingredients.
- Gives you worksheets on which to collate the necessary foods for your short term-food storage.
- Provides eight checklists to give you suggestions for kits to help your family in crises large or small
- Shows you how to determine your water needs and how to provide for those needs for your family

This workbook is, as far as I know, the only product of its kind that walks you through each step of the process to building your own stockpile of foods that your family will eat and enjoy. The worksheets provide you with step-by-step instructions, and give you space to fill out your information, to tailor this journey to meet your own particular needs. Have a gluten issue? No problem! You will choose your own shelf-stable foods that your family already eats. Really don't care for meat? No one's going to suggest that you eat it. Want to provide most of your own fruits and veggies from your own garden? Go right ahead. This workbook allows you to build this journey for YOUR family from start to finish. The checklists are meant as suggestions. Cross out the items you don't think you need. Add items in the extra spaces provided. Tailor this specifically for you.

In order to make full use of this workbook you need to have access to a copy of the book *A Year Without the Grocery Store*. If you are a member of the *Kindle Owners Lending Library*, you can read it free through there. If you aren't a member, you can purchase it either on Kindle or buy a paperback through Amazon here. Many of the assignments in the book are worked through in this workbook. Everything in this workbook will make much more sense if you've read through the book already or if you read it while working through the workbook. The order of this workbook parallels the chapters in the book.

Take your time to go through this workbook. This isn't a book that you can read in 48 hours and be done. This will take time, thought, effort, and sometimes money. Don't get overwhelmed with one aspect. Everything that you do, every step that you take, every skill that you learn makes you more prepared than you otherwise would have been.

Some helpful tips to using this workbook:

1.) Print this workbook out, punch holes in it, and put it in a notebook.
2.) Purchase some page protectors and fine tip whiteboard markers You'll want them part way through the workbook.
3.) Always start with pencil. You can go back later and use a pen or marker.
4.) Take this one day at a time. If this workbook takes you a week, great. If it takes you six months, that's fine! Don't stress over it. What's important is the direction you're going, not how fast you get there.
5.) Join our Facebook Group. You'll have to request to be added. Once I confirm that you've purchased this workbook, I'll confirm your request. The Facebook group has been set up to encourage one another on our journeys, to answer each other's questions, and to help each other plan.

Worksheets Pertaining to Chapter 2
of
A Year Without the Grocery Store

Foods from the Garden My Family Will Eat

This is a simple enough worksheet. I'm going to list off all of the typical vegetables, herbs, and some fruit grown in the continental United States. Circle the items your family will eat. Put a star by the foods you've never tried and actually try them!

This will help you when you go on to the next section of planning your garden. Please remember that this is not a comprehensive list of all foods grown in the ground (as opposed to those grown on trees or bushes). This is just the most common garden fruits, herbs, and veggies

Asparagus	Eggplant	Radish
Artichoke	Garlic	Rhubarb
Avocado	Ginger	Rosemary
Basil	Honeydew	Sage
Beans (black eye pea)	Kale	Spinach
Beans (bush)	Kohlrabi	Squash (acorn)
Beans (kidney)	Leek	Squash (butternut)
Beans (lima)	Lettuce (iceberg)	Squash (crookneck)
Beans (navy)	Lettuce (red leaf)	Squash (delicata)
Beans (pinto)	Lettuce (romaine)	Squash (spaghetti)
Beans (pole)	Mint (peppermint)	Squash (summer)
Beats	Mint (spearmint)	Strawberry
Broccoli	Mustard green	Sweet Potato
Brussel Sprouts	Onion	Tarragon
Cabbage	Okra	Thyme
Cantaloupe	Oregano	Tomato
Carrot	Parsley	Turnip
Cauliflower	Parsnip	Watermelon
Chamomile	Pea	Zucchini
Chives	Pepper	
Cilantro	Potato	
Cucumber	Pumpkin	

Having a garden tilled up and ready to plant is absolutely wonderful. The sense of accomplishment, even at just that first step, is huge.

But what do you do after you have your garden ready? Do you just throw seeds into the ground? Let's start with our A's in one section, like artichoke and asparagus. The next section is beans. Let's follow that with cauliflower!

Um . . . No. Having a garden takes planning. After you've filled out the section for what foods from the garden that my family will eat, then we can start working on this section of the workbook to plan your garden.

Each food takes up a different amount of space in your garden. You need to be sensitive to that. The best garden reference I've found for that is *The All New Square Foot Gardening*. It's a book I would highly recommend! It walks you through the most efficient way of planting your garden for the maximum use of your space.

Once you've decided on the foods that you want to plant, and determined how much space each of those plants require, then you decide if there are any plants that require special needs—like trellises. All of these will figure into your garden design.

On the following pages of graph paper I suggest that you start outlining your garden rows or garden beds with a sharpie marker, then fill in the key provided. Color a square and label what goes in the square next to it. Make sure that you mark and plan for any trellises.

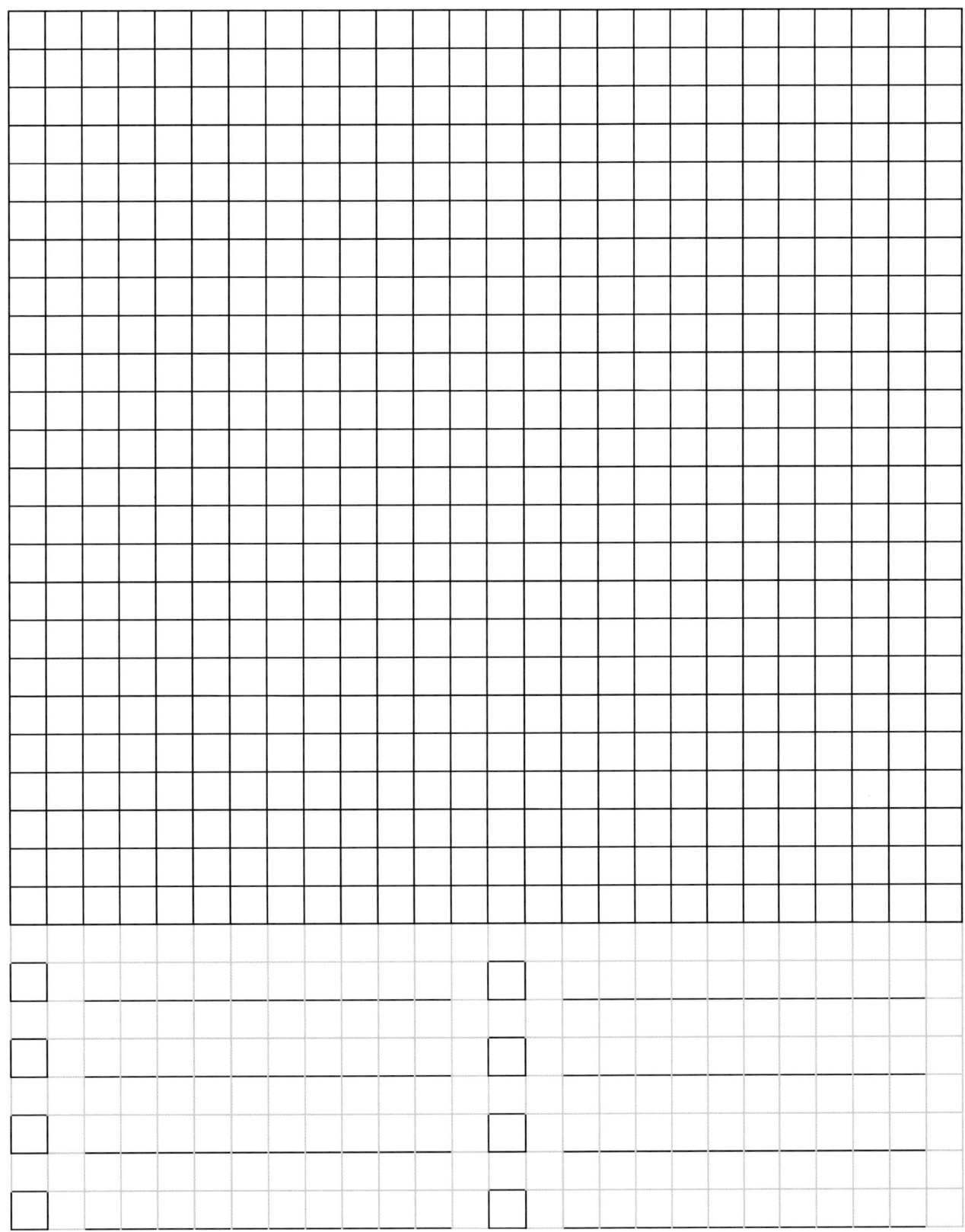

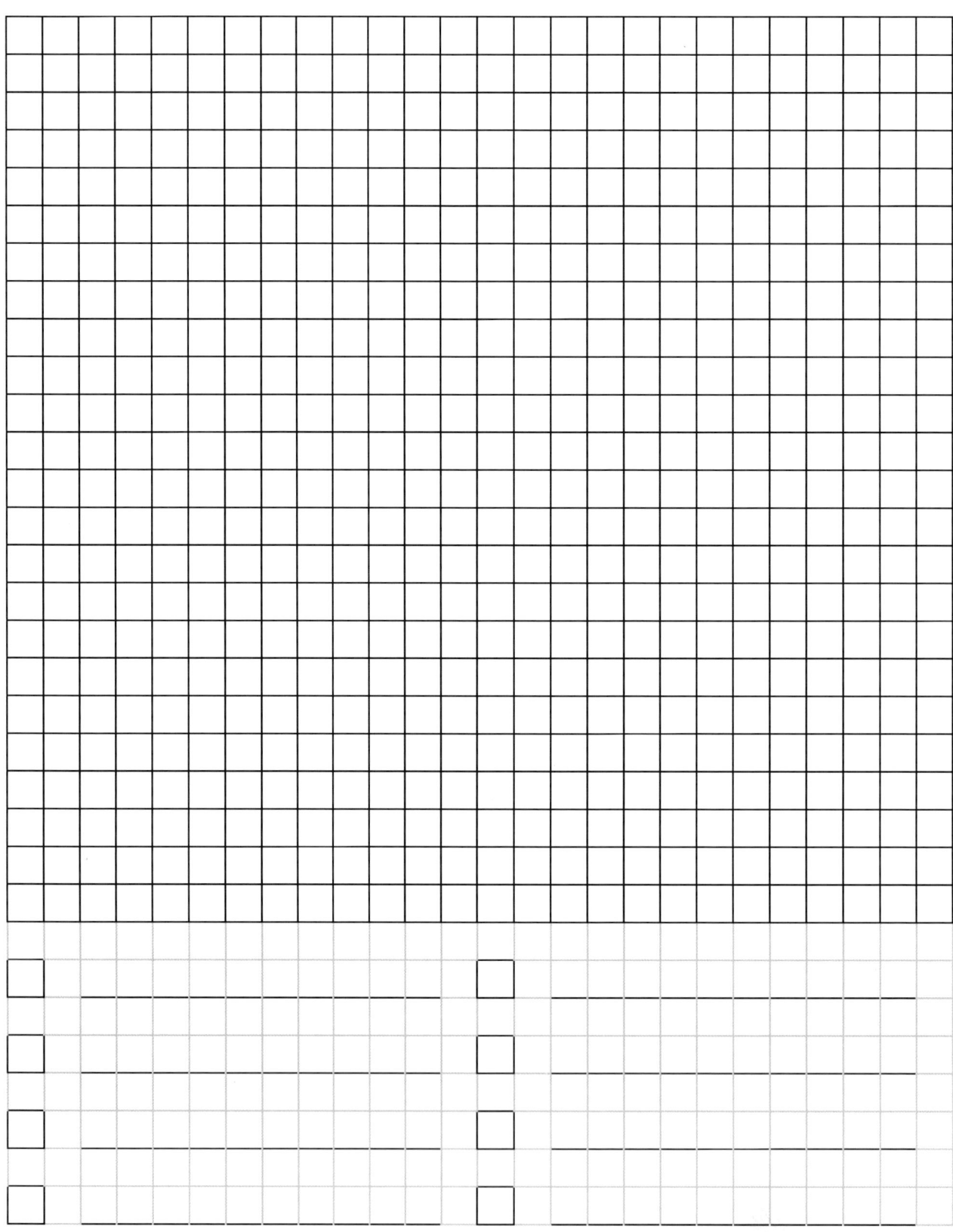

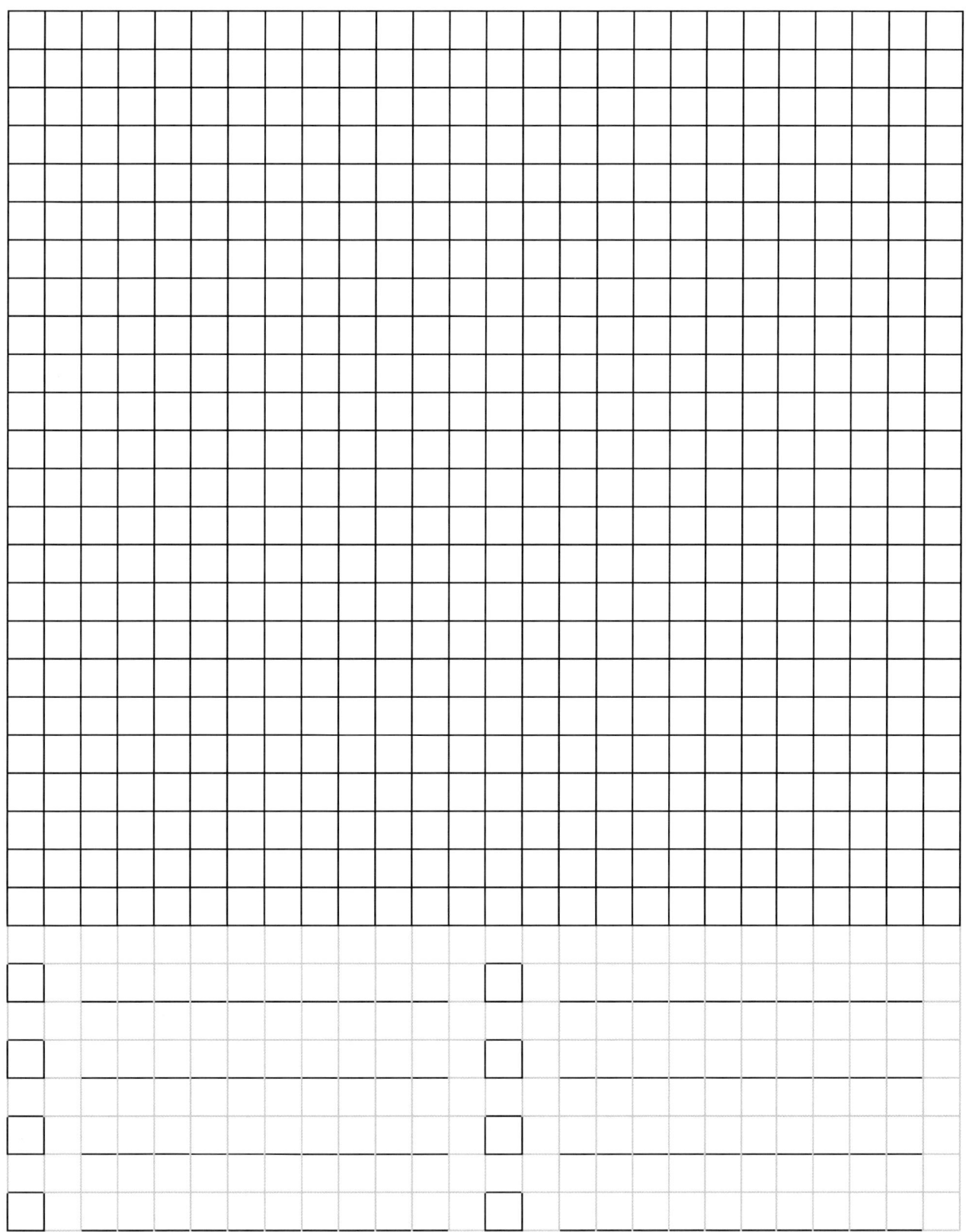

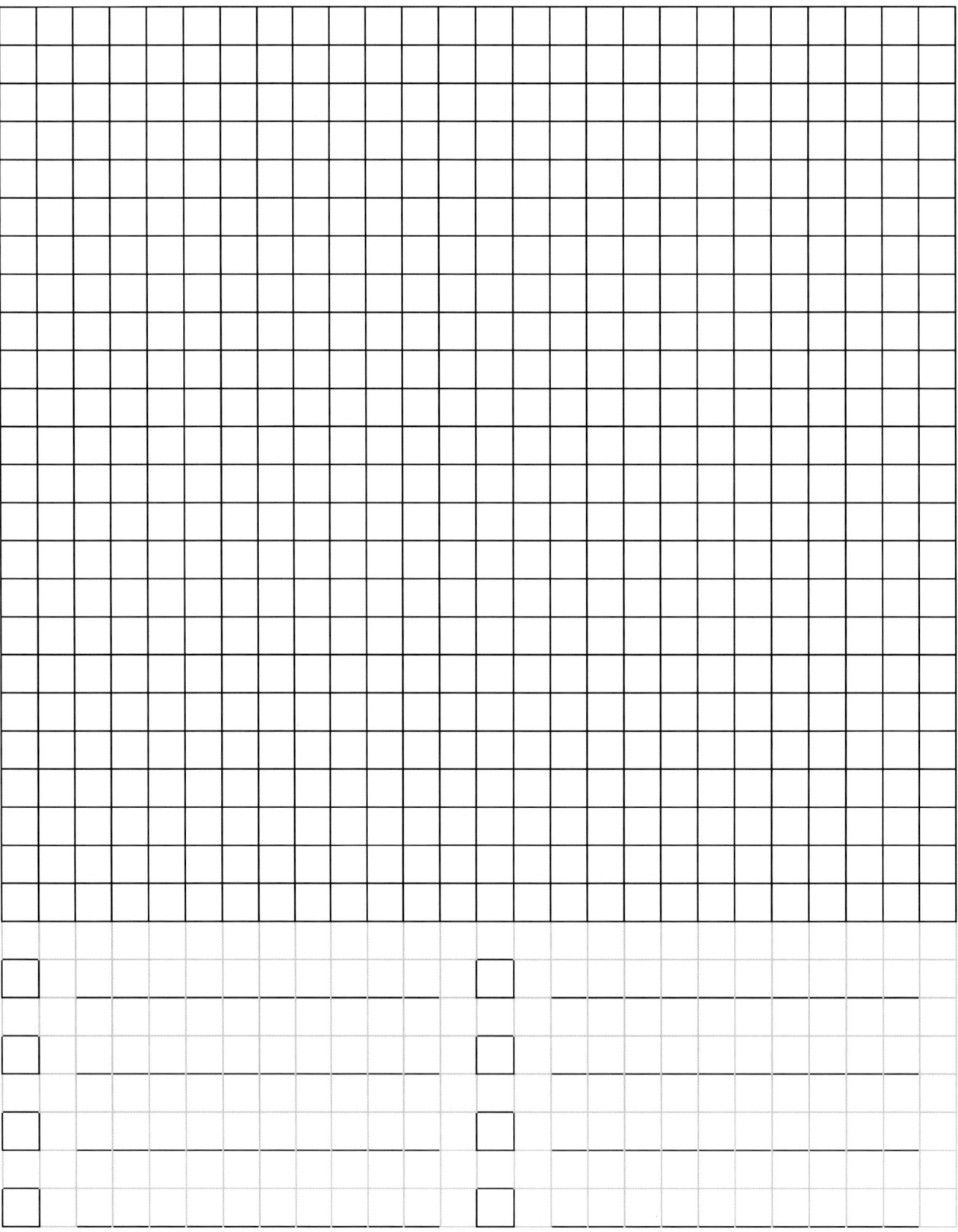

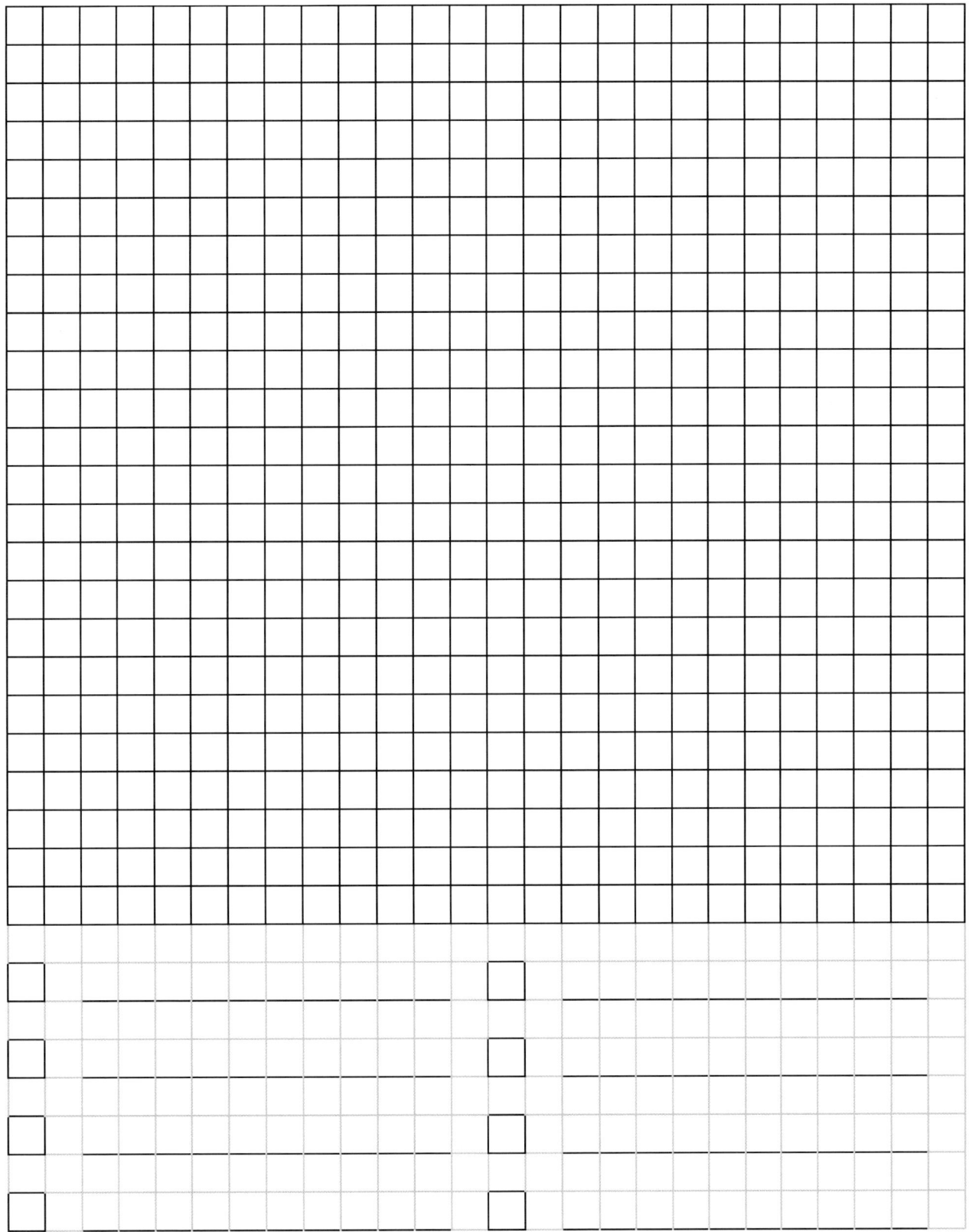

Garden Recap

One of the most important parts of planting a garden is doing a recap of your yearly garden. That may sound absolutely right on to you or it may sound way out of left field.

For many years I organized Thanksgiving Tea for the ladies of our church. Each year was good in different ways. One of the ways that I kept trying to improve on Tea was to do a recap. Each year, after the last table was put away and the floor was swept, whoever was working on Tea would sit down with me and recap the event. We would talk about what went well, what didn't go well, what we wanted to keep the same, and what we could improve upon. These things helped the next year's Tea to be better planned and enjoyed by all organizing and attending.

It's the same with your garden. Maybe all your tomatoes died this year, then you know you need to look into how to help your tomatoes thrive. What if your strawberries bloomed and you got a few small ones, but not a lot? Then maybe you need to look into strawberries. What if you tried making rhubarb jam and it was amazing! You'll want to note the recipe that you used and that you preserved the rhubarb by making jam.

Do NOT trust your memory on this. Just because you had 15 pints of rhubarb jam sitting on your shelf in September doesn't mean that you'll necessarily remember that come next April. Don't leave anything to chance. Write it down. Make notes. Dirty up the paper and mark it all up. You'll be so glad that you did when the next year rolls around!

Garden Recap From 20_____ Season: _____

I planted (fruit, vegetable, or herb)	How many I planted	How many I harvested	I preserved it by (freezing, canning, dehydrating)	How many pints / quarts	I need to do this many more	I had this many extra	What to do I need to research to improve?

Garden Recap From 20_____ Season: _____

I planted (fruit, vegetable, or herb)	How many I planted	How many I harvested	I preserved it by (freezing, canning, dehydrating)	How many pints / quarts	I need to do this many more	I had this many extra	What to do I need to research to improve?

Garden Recap From 20_____ Season: _____

I planted (fruit, vegetable, or herb)	How many I planted	How many I harvested	I preserved it by (freezing, canning, dehydrating)	How many pints / quarts	I need to do this many more	I had this many extra	What to do I need to research to improve?

Garden Recap From 20_____ Season: _____

I planted (fruit, vegetable, or herb)	How many I planted	How many I harvested	I preserved it by (freezing, canning, dehydrating)	How many pints / quarts	I need to do this many more	I had this many extra	What to do I need to research to improve?

Garden Recap From 20_____ Season: _____

I planted (fruit, vegetable, or herb)	How many I planted	How many I harvested	I preserved it by (freezing, canning, dehydrating)	How many pints / quarts	I need to do this many more	I had this many extra	What to do I need to research to improve?

Garden Recap From 20_____ Season: _____

I planted (fruit, vegetable, or herb)	How many I planted	How many I harvested	I preserved it by (freezing, canning, dehydrating)	How many pints / quarts	I need to do this many more	I had this many extra	What to do I need to research to improve?

Garden Recap From 20____   Season: _____

I planted (fruit, vegetable, or herb)	How many I planted	How many I harvested	I preserved it by (freezing, canning, dehydrating)	How many pints / quarts	I need to do this many more	I had this many extra	What to do I need to research to improve?

Garden Recap From 20_____ Season: _____

I planted (fruit, vegetable, or herb)	How many I planted	How many I harvested	I preserved it by (freezing, canning, dehydrating)	How many pints / quarts	I need to do this many more	I had this many extra	What to do I need to research to improve?

Long-Term
Food Storage Spreadsheet

When we're talking about food storage, starting with a garden is important, but getting your long-term storage off the ground and running is so important. I am going to suggest that you slip this sheet into a sheet protector and use a dry erase marker to keep track of what you have. It will change all the time, so you don't want to use pen. Erasing pencil marks can also leave holes in your paper, so dry erase marker on a sheet protector is an easy way to go to keep track of your stash.

Food	I want	I have	Need to buy	Cheapest @
Apple Cider Vinegar				
Beans (dried black)				
Beans (dried kidney)				
Beans (dried navy)				
Beans (dried pinto)				
Corn (dried)				
Grain Alcohol				
Honey				
Milk (powdered non-fat)				
Oats (quick)				
Oats (rolled)				
Pasta (linguini)				
Pasta (macaroni)				
Pasta (spaghetti)				
Pasta (spiral)				
Pasta (manicotti)				
Potato flakes				

Food	I want	I have	Need to Buy	Cheapest @
Salt				
Sugar				
Wheat berries				
White rice				
Vanilla				

Planning and Purchasing Long-Term Food Storage

In order to help you acquire the long-term food storage that you set as your goal in the last section, this section will help you compare prices and determine where you are going to get your best buy for bulk items.

The best priced bulk items can be found at two places: LDS Cannery and Azure Standard.

LDS Cannery sells twenty-five-pound bags of white wheat and red wheat. Everything else they sell is in #10 cans. If you order online, instead of at a cannery, you may have to purchase your #10 cans in cases of six. Each month LDS Cannery has sales on specified items. You can call your local LDS Cannery and ask them to add you to their email list. They will email you each month with which items are on sale. The sales will be the same across all locations.

A list of LDS Cannery locations can be found here:
https://providentliving.lds.org/self-reliance/food-storage/home-storage-center-locations?lang=eng.

The LDS Cannery prices can be found here:
https://providentliving.lds.org/self-reliance/food-storage/home-storage-center-order-form?lang=eng Don't be spooked by the prices! Some might seem high, but please remember that some of these are cases of six ten-pound cans.

My nearest LDS Cannery is:

Address: _____

Phone number: _____

Hours: _____

Azure Standard will need a little more explanation. Azure Standard is a mail order or monthly delivery co-op.

You can purchase many of the items and have them shipped to you. Your other option in order to be able to purchase the gamut of the products is to sign up for a drop.

If you want to purchase from Azure Standard you will need to sign up for an account. This is FREE. You aren't obligated to order ever, let alone on a monthly basis, but you are able to order on a monthly basis if you'd like. You order only when you want to order.
Signing up is simple. Go to http://www.azurestandard.com, and sign up for an account.

Part of signing up for Azure Standard is signing up for a drop. You don't have to use the drop, but unless things have changed you have to sign up for a drop. They will help you find the nearest drops to your home or work.

Once you've signed up for Azure Standard, and for a drop, you can browse all their items and see their prices. You'll add items to your cart. You still aren't obligated to purchase any of those items. Those items won't be sent to your drop unless you "check out." Once you do "check out" you can change your order at any time up until the deadline for your drop. You can add things to your order. You can remove things from you order. You could even completely delete your order. If you want to order though, you must make sure that you "check out" before your cut off. You can always find this at the top of any Azure pages. Mine currently says "Cut Off 16d 22h 22m," so I have a little over two weeks until my drop deadline or "cut off."

Your drop cut off is always four weeks from your last drop cut off. My delivery date is always one week from my cut off date. Yours might be 6 days or 8 days, but it will be around one week.

Coming up to your order cut off and your drop date you'll probably hear from someone who is called your "drop coordinator." This is the person who is in charge of making sure everyone who wants to order places an order on time. They make sure everyone who orders knows the date and time of their drop. If you forget your drop (I've done this once, oops), your drop coordinator will call you. They also organize the unloading of the truck.

The day of your drop you'll need to arrive at your specified place at the specified time. If you can't pick up your order, you'll need to send someone in your place to get it. As you get to know people from your drop, sometimes one of them may be willing to pick it up for you if you can't make it.

Azure has almost everything that I need for long-term food storage. They also have amazing prices to boot.

On the next pages you'll see a spreadsheet so that you can compare the prices for Azure, LDS Cannery, and other local-to-you bulk places. This should help you determine where to order from. Keep in mind that both Azure and LDS Cannery have sales each month, so that should affect your purchases.

Food	Azure Price	LDS Cannery Price	Local Bulk	Other
Apple Cider Vinegar				
Beans (dried black)				
Beans (dried kidney)				
Beans (dried navy)				
Beans (dried pinto)				
Corn (dried)				
Grain Alcohol				
Honey				
Milk (powdered non-fat)				
Oats (quick)				
Oats (rolled)				
Pasta (linguini)				
Pasta (macaroni)				
Pasta (spaghetti)				
Pasta (spiral)				
Pasta (manicotti)				
Potato flakes				
Salt				
Sugar				
Wheat berries				
White rice				
Vanilla				

Worksheets Pertaining to Chapter 3
of
A Year Without the Grocery Store

I remember the first time I sealed oats, wheat, beans, and rice in Mylar bags. I was afraid that I was going to do it all wrong and lose all my food. However, I have some good news! I didn't lose any of the food that I sealed up, and I'm going to walk you through the very same, simple process I used.

1.) Grab your five to six-gallon bucket with a lid, a six-gallon Mylar bag, a 2000cc oxygen absorber, a 2 foot or longer length of 2x4 (or 1x4), and an iron. Start by plugging the iron in and letting it heat up.

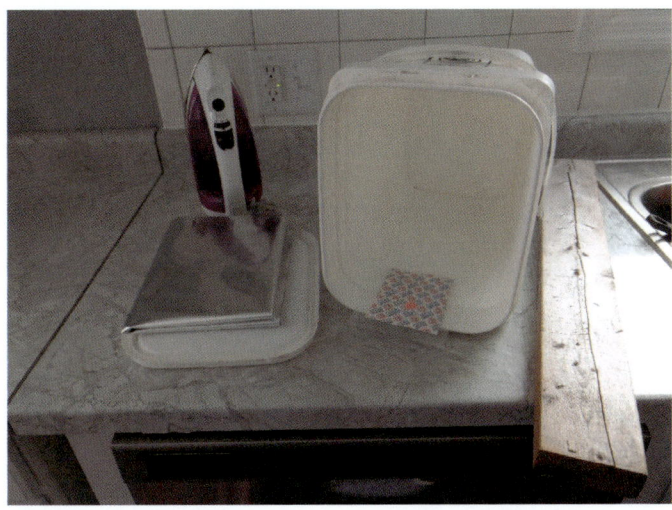

2.) Stand the Mylar bag up in the bucket and pour whatever it is that you want to preserve into the bag.

3.) When the bucket looks just about full, you'll want to bounce it up and down and then twist it back and forth quickly. This will help the contents to settle. Do this several times and add more. Once it's all settled and it's filled within two inches to the top, lay the 2x4 across the bucket.

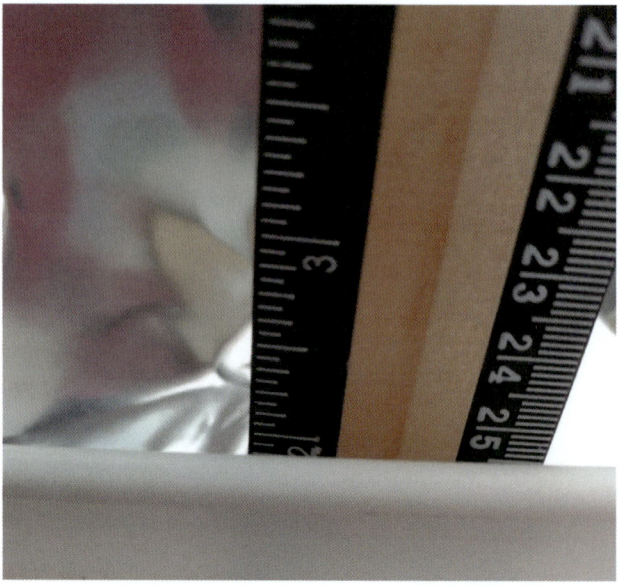

4.) Pull the Mylar bag up, straighten it as much as is possible and pull it across the 2x4. You're going to iron the bag, all but two inches across. Keep it as flat as possible while doing this.

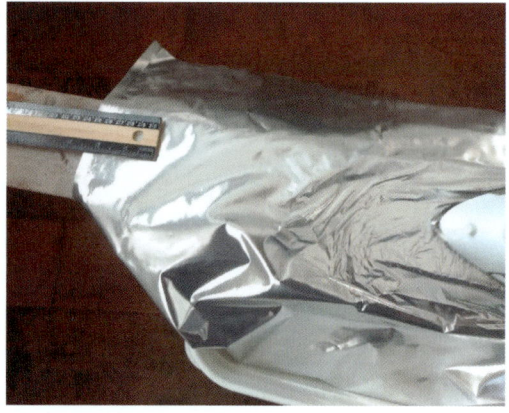

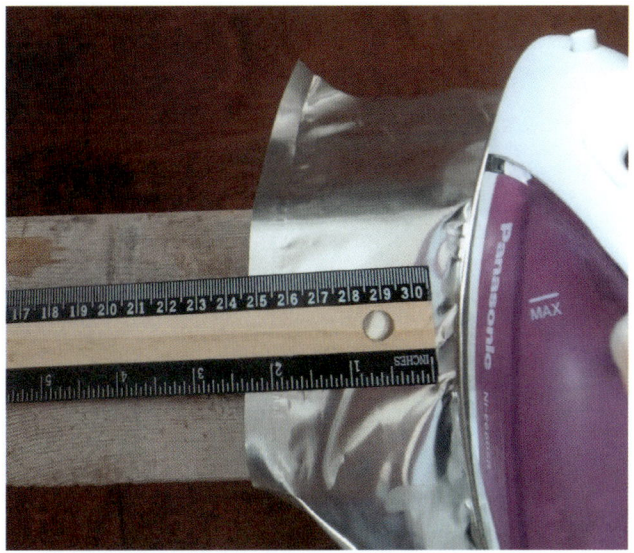

5.) Pull the bag back up, and then push it down into the bucket to squeeze as much air out as possible.   If you are using single sealed oxygen absorbers (which you can find here: https://amzn.to/2lFgwa1), this is when you will open the single oxygen absorber. Stuff it through the 2 inches that you left open.

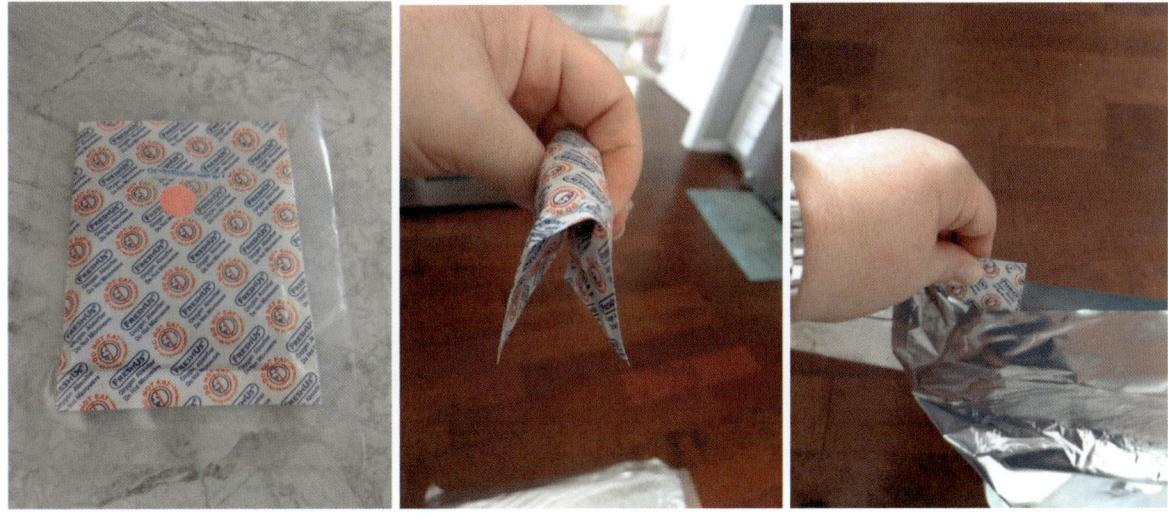

6.) Pull the bag back up and straighten it over the 2x4 and iron the rest of the way across.

7.) Fold the bag back down. Stuff it into the bucket and place the lid on.

8.) Write the date and the contents on the lid.

And you're done!

If you do NOT purchase single sealed oxygen absorbers, then do steps 1-4 for every bucket that you are going to do. If you have ten buckets that you're doing then do all ten buckets up through step five BEFORE you do step six. Then you'll need to do step six as quickly as possible so that the oxygen absorbers don't lose their potency.

Follow the rest of the steps 7 and 8, and you'll be done.

Worksheets Pertaining to Chapter 4
of
A Year Without the Grocery Store

Planning Short-Term Food Storage

When planning for short-term food storage it's always easiest to start by making a list of meals that your family already eats.

1.) On the following pages list as many breakfast, lunch, and dinner ideas as you can (but a minimum of ten to twelve) that your family already enjoys. Your family is a great resource to ask for their favorite meals.

2.) For snacks, desserts, and drinks list as many as you can come up with.

3.) Once you've done that, go through each one listed and determine which meals would work well as a food storage meal. Look for a couple of common denominators that will help determine if any of the meals that you've written down will translate into food storage meals. Look for meals that:

    a.) Most of the ingredients are boxed

    b.) Most of the ingredients are canned

    c.) The meal is easy to make

    d.) For the ingredients that aren't boxed or canned, can you find a shelf stable substitute like freeze dried meats or cheeses?

4.) From that list choose your favorite seven breakfast, lunch, and dinner ideas. Include your favorite five to seven snacks, desserts, and drinks. Put a star by them.

Breakfasts

1.)

2.)

3.)

4.)

5.)

6.)

7.)

8.)

9.)

10.)

11.)

12.)

13.)

14.)

15.)

16.)

17.)

18.)

19.)

20.)

21.)

Lunches

1.)

2.)

3.)

4.)

5.)

6.)

7.)

8.)

9.)

10.)

11.)

12.)

13.)

14.)

15.)

16.)

17.)

18.)

19.)

20.)

Dinners

1.)

2.)

3.)

4.)

5.)

6.)

7.)

8.)

9.)

10.)

11.)

12.)

13.)

14.)

15.)

16.)

17.)

18.)

19.)

20.)

Snacks

1.)

2.)

3.)

4.)

5.)

6.)

7.)

8.)

9.)

10.)

11.)

12.)

13.)

14.)

15.)

16.)

17.)

18.)

19.)

20.)

Desserts

1.)

2.)

3.)

4.)

5.)

6.)

7.)

8.)

9.)

10.)

11.)

12.)

13.)

14.)

15.)

16.)

17.)

18.)

19.)

20.)

Drinks

1.)

2.)

3.)

4.)

5.)

6.)

7.)

8.)

9.)

10.)

You're well on your way to having your short-term food storage planned! Now we're going to take the next step to plan your short-term food storage.

Determine how many weeks of food storage you believe is best for your family.

My family needs _____ weeks of short-term food storage.

Take the starred meals, snacks, and other items from the *Planning Short-Term Food Storage Part I* worksheets and list the name of each meal on the top of each page. There are seven breakfast pages. Put the name of your seven breakfasts one on the top of each breakfast page.

Once you've done that, go back to your first recipe. On the lines below the recipe name, write one ingredient per line, making sure to list each ingredient needed to make that recipe for your family.

The second column of the chart should be filled in with how much of that ingredient you need to make that recipe once.

The third column is the number you listed above on this page in the "weeks of short-term food storage." Multiply the second column by the third columns and put that result in the last column. This is the amount of that ingredient that you should be storing for that given recipe. One breakfast recipe is done for you as an example.

Once you've done that then go back and list out the ingredients in each meal or snack, or drink etc.

The number you put in the blank above is the number you will fill in under "short-term storage goal in weeks."

This will give you the basis for what you're going to want to stock up on.

Breakfast:

Breakfast Casserole

Ingredient	Amount for one recipe	Short Term food storage goal in weeks	Total Amount needed
Freeze Dried hash browns	3 C	12	36 C
Powdered Eggs	1 ½ C	12	16 C
Freeze Dried Sausage Crumbles	1 C	12	12 C
Milk Powder	3 T	12	1 ¾ C
Mustard Powder	1 T	12	¾ C
Freeze Dried Cheese	1 C	12	12 C
Very Warm Water	2 C	12	24 C
Directions on back			

Breakfast:

_____

Ingredient	Amount for one recipe	Short Term food storage goal in weeks	Total Amount needed

Breakfast:

_____

Ingredient	Amount for one recipe	Short Term food storage goal in weeks	Total Amount needed

Breakfast:

_____

Ingredient	Amount for one recipe	Short Term food storage goal in weeks	Total Amount needed

Breakfast:

_____

Ingredient	Amount for one recipe	Short Term food storage goal in weeks	Total Amount needed

Breakfast:

_____

Ingredient	Amount for one recipe	Short Term food storage goal in weeks	Total Amount needed

Breakfast:

_____

Ingredient	Amount for one recipe	Short Term food storage goal in weeks	Total Amount needed

Breakfast:

_____

Ingredient	Amount for one recipe	Short Term food storage goal in weeks	Total Amount needed

Lunch:

_____

Ingredient	Amount for one recipe	Short Term food storage goal in weeks	Total Amount needed

Lunch:

_____

Ingredient	Amount for one recipe	Short Term food storage goal in weeks	Total Amount needed

Lunch:

_____

Ingredient	Amount for one recipe	Short Term food storage goal in weeks	Total Amount needed

Lunch:

_____

Ingredient	Amount for one recipe	Short Term food storage goal in weeks	Total Amount needed

Lunch:

_____

Ingredient	Amount for one recipe	Short Term food storage goal in weeks	Total Amount needed

Lunch:

_____

Ingredient	Amount for one recipe	Short Term food storage goal in weeks	Total Amount needed

Lunch:

_____

Ingredient	Amount for one recipe	Short Term food storage goal in weeks	Total Amount needed

Dinner:

_____

Ingredient	Amount for one recipe	Short Term food storage goal in weeks	Total Amount needed

Dinner:

_____

Ingredient	Amount for one recipe	Short Term food storage goal in weeks	Total Amount needed

Dinner:

_____

Ingredient	Amount for one recipe	Short Term food storage goal in weeks	Total Amount needed

Dinner:

_____

Ingredient	Amount for one recipe	Short Term food storage goal in weeks	Total Amount needed

Dinner:

_____

Ingredient	Amount for one recipe	Short Term food storage goal in weeks	Total Amount needed

Dinner:

_____

Ingredient	Amount for one recipe	Short Term food storage goal in weeks	Total Amount needed

Dinner:

_____

Ingredient	Amount for one recipe	Short Term food storage goal in weeks	Total Amount needed

Snack:

_____

Ingredient	Amount for one recipe	Short Term food storage goal in weeks	Total Amount needed

Snack:

_____

Ingredient	Amount for one recipe	Short Term food storage goal in weeks	Total Amount needed

Snack:

_____

Ingredient	Amount for one recipe	Short Term food storage goal in weeks	Total Amount needed

Snack:

_____

Ingredient	Amount for one recipe	Short Term food storage goal in weeks	Total Amount needed

Snack:

_____

Ingredient	Amount for one recipe	Short Term food storage goal in weeks	Total Amount needed

Snack:

_____

Ingredient	Amount for one recipe	Short Term food storage goal in weeks	Total Amount needed

Snack:

_____

Ingredient	Amount for one recipe	Short Term food storage goal in weeks	Total Amount needed

Dessert:

_____

Ingredient	Amount for one recipe	Short Term food storage goal in weeks	Total Amount needed

Dessert:

_____

Ingredient	Amount for one recipe	Short Term food storage goal in weeks	Total Amount needed

Dessert:

_____

Ingredient	Amount for one recipe	Short Term food storage goal in weeks	Total Amount needed

Dessert:

_____

Ingredient	Amount for one recipe	Short Term food storage goal in weeks	Total Amount needed

Dessert:

_____

Ingredient	Amount for one recipe	Short Term food storage goal in weeks	Total Amount needed

Dessert:

_____

Ingredient	Amount for one recipe	Short Term food storage goal in weeks	Total Amount needed

Dessert:

_____

Ingredient	Amount for one recipe	Short Term food storage goal in weeks	Total Amount needed

Drink:

_____

Ingredient	Amount for one recipe	Short Term food storage goal in weeks	Total Amount needed

Drink: _____

Ingredient	Amount for one recipe	Short Term food storage goal in weeks	Total Amount needed

Drink:

_____

Ingredient	Amount for one recipe	Short Term food storage goal in weeks	Total Amount needed

Drink: _____

Ingredient	Amount for one recipe	Short Term food storage goal in weeks	Total Amount needed

Drink:

_____

Ingredient	Amount for one recipe	Short Term food storage goal in weeks	Total Amount needed

Drink: _____

Ingredient	Amount for one recipe	Short Term food storage goal in weeks	Total Amount needed

Drink:

_____

Ingredient	Amount for one recipe	Short Term food storage goal in weeks	Total Amount needed

Drink: _____

Ingredient	Amount for one recipe	Short Term food storage goal in weeks	Total Amount needed

All the numbers that you've gathered thus far are awesome; however, they do you no good unless you have a master list of all of your ingredients. This list should include how much you have, how much more you need, and how much extra you have of any given ingredient.

Here's an example excerpt from my personal spreadsheet.

Ingredients	Have	Need
Baking Powder (in cups)	3	2 3/4
Basil	5	1.5
Black Beans	77	5
Bean Soup Mix (in cups)	144	72
Beef, FD	60	0
butter powder	12	4.5
Carrots, FD	12	0
Celery, FD	12	6
Cheese, FD	30	-6
Chicken, FD Shredded	90	18
Chili beans (in 15 oz cans)	25	13
Chili Powder (in Cups)	12	3
Coconut Oil (in cups)	12	3.75
Corn (Dried)	30	6

My list changes on a weekly basis. I update it as I have time. Doing it on a weekly basis would be better.

I would suggest doing it this way: take your first recipe and, using a pencil, go down your ingredients one at a time and list the given ingredient with its amount that you need on the appropriate spreadsheet that follows this instruction page. As you move onto new recipes, check to see if the ingredient is already on the list before adding it as a new line. The point of this exercise is to collate all of your ingredients. This will give you a master list of what you need and what areas you need to focus your efforts on.

Once you have all your ingredients collated, I would highly suggest writing your ingredients in pen and slipping the page into a page protector. Then write your totals on the outside of the page protector using thin tipped white board markers. This will both protect the paper and allow you to easily change your totals.

Running Tally of Ingredients

Dry Ingredients

Ingredient	Amount Needed	Amount I have	Need to Buy

Running Tally of Ingredients

Dry Ingredients

Ingredient	Amount Needed	Amount I have	Need to Buy

Running Tally of Ingredients

Dry Ingredients

Ingredient	Amount Needed	Amount I have	Need to Buy

Running Tally of Ingredients

Canned Ingredients

Ingredient	Amount Needed	Amount I have	Need to Buy

Running Tally of Ingredients

Canned Ingredients

Ingredient	Amount Needed	Amount I have	Need to Buy

Running Tally of Ingredients

Canned Ingredients

Ingredient	Amount Needed	Amount I have	Need to Buy

Running Tally of Ingredients

Freeze Dried Foods

Ingredient	Amount Needed	Amount I have	Need to Buy

Running Tally of Ingredients

Freeze Dried Foods

Ingredient	Amount Needed	Amount I have	Need to Buy

Running Tally of Ingredients

Freeze Dried Foods

Ingredient	Amount Needed	Amount I have	Need to Buy

Running Tally of Other Ingredients

Ingredient	Amount Needed	Amount I have	Need to Buy

Running Tally of Other Ingredients

Ingredient	Amount Needed	Amount I have	Need to Buy

Running Tally of Other Ingredients

Ingredient	Amount Needed	Amount I have	Need to Buy

Worksheets Pertaining to Chapter 5
of
A Year Without the Grocery Store

72 Hour Kit Worksheet

Food is the backbone of our seventy-two-hour kit. I generally plan the same meal for breakfast all three days. I do the same for lunch. Dinner I will vary from day to day. So when you are planning your meals below, decide if you want to have the same meal or different meals.

I keep my seventy-two-hour kit filled with easily cooked food or no cook food. I also keep it in a separate tote marked "seventy-two-hour food kit" along with all the paper bowls, plates, utensils, and a way to cook the food. This way, whether I'm home or whether I'm leaving, all the food is in one kit in one location, and I don't need to worry.

Breakfast Ideas - Choose one to three
- ❏ Oatmeal
- ❏ Grits
- ❏ Cold Cereal
- ❏ Granola Bars
- ❏ Boxed Pastries
- ❏ Freeze Dried Hash Browns
- ❏ _____
- ❏ _____
- ❏ _____

Breakfast Drink Ideas - Choose one to three
- ❏ Hot chocolate
- ❏ Instant Coffee or Regular coffee and French Press
- ❏ Tang
- ❏ _____
- ❏ _____

Lunch Ideas - Choose one to three

- ❏ Crackers and meat (potted deviled ham, turkey, or chicken canned tuna or salmon, or pepperonis)
- ❏ Macaroni and Cheese
- ❏ Spam and Beans
- ❏ Canned Soup
- ❏ Sandwiches (PB&J or something else not needing refrigeration)

Dinner Ideas - Choose one to three

- ❏ Beans and rice
- ❏ Spaghetti
- ❏ Boxed dinners such as Tuna Helper (™)
- ❏ Soup over rice
- ❏ Salmon or tuna patties and fruit

Lunch and Dinner Drink Ideas

- ❏ Drink Sticks
- ❏ Instant iced tea
- ❏ Water bottles
- ❏ Instant Coffee

Day One Menu

Breakfast:

Lunch:

Dinner:

Day Two Menu

Breakfast:

Lunch:

Dinner:

Day Three Menu

Breakfast:

Lunch:

Dinner:

Ingredient	Have	Need

Clothes
- ❏ One to two changes of clothes

Hygiene zip top bag - I use quart size bag and all these fit in just fine)
- ❏ Soap
- ❏ Travel Shampoo
- ❏ Travel deodorant
- ❏ Wash cloth
- ❏ Comb
- ❏ Hair Bands
- ❏ Feminine Products (for ladies)
- ❏ Travel package of hand wipes
- ❏ Mini Kleenex
- ❏ Toothbrush
- ❏ Travel size toothpaste
- ❏ Travel Baby Powder
- ❏ Lotion
- ❏ Floss
- ❏ Travel Q-tips
- ❏ Emergency Blanket
- ❏ Hand/foot warmers

Travel Help
- ❏ Headlamp
- ❏ Knife
- ❏ Leatherman
- ❏ Cigarette lighter
- ❏ Waterproof matches
- ❏ Work Gloves
- ❏ Two-Person Tent

- ❑ Bandanas
- ❑ Tarps
- ❑ Cordage
- ❑ Pocket Chain Saw
- ❑ Hatchet

For Kids

- ❑ Something fun to do
- ❑ "Lovie" or stuffed animal
- ❑ Composition book or other writing drawing book
- ❑ Colored Pencils
- ❑ Clicker Pencils
- ❑ Book to read
- ❑ Small game or card game to play

Everyday Carry Checklist

Basic Items

- ❏ Knife - check your state's laws on what is permissible or not
- ❏ Flashlight
- ❏ Pepper spray or other personal defense
- ❏ Umbrella
- ❏ Small notebook and pen
- ❏
- ❏
- ❏
- ❏

Personal Care Items

- ❏ Hand lotion
- ❏ Sunscreen
- ❏ Baby powder
- ❏ Hand sanitizer
- ❏ Lip balm
- ❏ Feminine hygiene items for the ladies
- ❏ Facial tissues
- ❏ Floss
- ❏ Hairband and/or clip for the ladies
- ❏ Comb
- ❏ Extra pair of glasses
- ❏ Nail clippers
- ❏ Band Aid
- ❏ Small scissors and yarn needle
- ❏ Eyeglass repair kit (if you have glasses)
- ❏ Extra pair of undergarments
- ❏
- ❏

Preparedness Items

- ❑ Cigarette lighter (I wrap mine with duct tape)
- ❑ Heavy duty shoe laces
- ❑ Magnifying glass
- ❑ Mini sewing kit
- ❑ Mirror
- ❑ Strong flashlight
- ❑ Whistle
- ❑
- ❑

First Aid

- ❑ Non-latex gloves
- ❑ More band aids
- ❑ Advil
- ❑ Aspirin
- ❑ Advil PM
- ❑ Tylenol
- ❑ Bandana
- ❑ "Neo to Go" - a sprayable Neosporin
- ❑ Large bandages
- ❑ Large ace wrap with safety pin
- ❑ Wound seal powder
- ❑ Super glue
- ❑ Benadryl cooling spray
- ❑ Arnica Montana
- ❑ Small roll of first aid tape
- ❑ Steri strips
- ❑
- ❑

Food

- ❑ Peppermints
- ❑ Cinnamon hard candy
- ❑ Misc. hard candies
- ❑ Gum
- ❑ Protein bars
- ❑

Our seventy-two-hour food kit also doubles as food for our power outage kit. But you need so much more than just food for your power outage kit. When we organize our power outage supplies, we separate them two ways. We use a large black tote with all of our power outage cooking items. We use a similar tote with six smaller clear totes inside it to keep our other power outage items organized.

Power Outage Cooking Tote
- ❏ Camp Stove
- ❏ Single burner butane stove
- ❏ Butane canisters
- ❏ Matches
- ❏ Egg beaters
- ❏ Hand crank mini food processor
- ❏ Can openers
- ❏ French press coffee pot
- ❏ Hand crank coffee grinder
- ❏ Hand chopper
- ❏ Hand crank grain grinder

Power Outage Black Tote

Subtote One - Lighting
- ❏ Tea Lights
- ❏ Electric tea lights (for night lights)
- ❏ Extra matches
- ❏ Several hand crank flashlights
- ❏ Extra larger candles
- ❏ Headlamp
- ❏ 1000 hour candle

Subtote Two - Cooling
- ❑ Cooling towels - 1 per person
- ❑ Battery operated fans
- ❑ D Batteries (for fans)

Subtote Three - Mending
- ❑ Thread (in multiple colors)
- ❑ Needles
- ❑ Patches

Subtote Four - Hygiene
- ❑ Several Hand Sanitizers
- ❑ Lysol Wipes
- ❑ Baby Wipes (for sponge baths)
- ❑ Hair bands
- ❑ Combs

Subtote Five - Communications
- ❑ Battery Powered Radio
- ❑ Walkie Talkies
- ❑ Hand Crank Radio
- ❑ Ham Radio
- ❑ Extra Batteries for radio and walkie talkies

Subtote Six - Heat
- ❑ Hand warmers
- ❑ Foot warmers
- ❑ Compact blankets
- ❑ Emergency blankets

Car Checklist

Food
- ❏ Liquid - Water in glass or Mylar pouches, juice boxes, or other liquids
- ❏ Snacks
  - ❏ Trail mix pouches
  - ❏ Nut packs
  - ❏ Tuna fish pouches with spoons
  - ❏ Cheese crackers
  - ❏ Meat sticks
  - ❏ Granola bars
  - ❏ Hard candies
  - ❏ Peppermints (for nausea or energy)
  - ❏ Freeze-dried fruits & veggies
  - ❏ Beef jerky

Navigation
- ❏ Paper map
- ❏ GPS

Personal Items for each person
- ❏ Walking shoes & socks (if not wearing)
- ❏ Change of undergarments
- ❏ Poncho
- ❏ Hygiene Kit
  - ❏ Travel shampoo
  - ❏ Travel soap
  - ❏ Washcloth
  - ❏ Travel deodorant
  - ❏ Hair bands (for girls/women with long hair)
  - ❏ Small comb
  - ❏ Travel toothbrush

- ❏ Travel toothpaste
- ❏ Floss
- ❏ Feminine hygiene (for those who need it)
- ❏ Comb
- ❏ Travel size package of hand wipes
- ❏ Mini package of tissues
- ❏ Baby powder
- ❏ Travel box of cotton swabs
- ❏ Hand warmers
- ❏ Space blanket

Mechanical Emergency Kit
- ❏ Jumper cables
- ❏ Emergency radio
- ❏ Crank flashlight
- ❏ Work gloves
- ❏ Car jack
- ❏ Flares
- ❏ Fix-a-Flat

Car Amenities
- ❏ Phone chargers
- ❏ Bug spray
- ❏ Sunburn care
- ❏ Picnic table cloths/blankets
- ❏ First-Aid kit
- ❏ Basic sewing kit
- ❏ Pad of paper
- ❏ Pen
- ❏ Sharpie
- ❏ Book to read
- ❏ Card game to play
- ❏ Baby wipes
- ❏ Toilet paper
- ❏ Two to three trash can liners
- ❏ Four to six gallon size Ziploc baggies
- ❏ Four to six quart size Ziploc baggies

Emergency Preparedness Items
- ❏ Berkey water bottle(s)
- ❏ Cooking kit
- ❏ Collapsible bowls
- ❏ Plastic utensils

- ❑ Small roll duct tape
- ❑ Tarps
- ❑ Work gloves
- ❑ Mallet
- ❑ Cordage
- ❑ Hatchet
- ❑ Flashlight varieties - at least three types
- ❑ Waterproof matches
- ❑ 1000-Hour candle
- ❑ Water treatment tablets
- ❑ Pocket chainsaw

Winter Items
- ❑ Cat litter
- ❑ Rock salt

Outdoor Tools and Other Needs for Self-Sufficiency

Garden Tools

- ❏ Hand tiller
- ❏ Trowel - Hori Hori
- ❏ Hoe
- ❏ Pick ax
- ❏ Shovel
- ❏ Gloves
- ❏ Chicken wire
- ❏ Wooden stakes
- ❏ Zip-ties
- ❏ Garden hand rake
- ❏ Full size rake
- ❏ Watering can
- ❏ Garden hose
- ❏ Full-size garden fork

Cutting Tools

- ❏ Saw
- ❏ Cross-cut saw
- ❏ Ax
- ❏ Wood splitting wedge
- ❏ Gardening shears
- ❏ Pruning shears

All Purpose Tools

- ❏ Wheelbarrow
- ❏ Ladder
- ❏ Burn cage

Sickness Tote Checklist

- ❑ One to two boxes of crackers
- ❑ Case of chicken noodle soup
- ❑ Case of chicken broth
- ❑ Two to three jars of applesauce
- ❑ One to two twelve-packs of ginger ale or lemon lime soda
- ❑ Peppermint tea
- ❑ Nausea medicines
- ❑ Fever medicines
- ❑ Cold & flu medicines
- ❑ Emergency-C or equivalent
- ❑ Essential oils or homeopathy

Leaving Home
for a Week or More
Checklist

- ❏ Does someone know where you're going, when you're supposed to arrive, and when you're due home?
- ❏ Did you put a stop on your mail and newspapers (if you still have them delivered)?
- ❏ Did you remember your medicines?
- ❏ Valuables hidden?
- ❏ Lights off?
- ❏ Oven/stove off?
- ❏ Iron/curling iron off?
- ❏ Power strips turned off?
- ❏ Hot water heater temperature adjusted?
- ❏ Water off to the house? (I've known people whose toilet overflowed while they were away! Oh what a mess to come home to!)
- ❏ Freeze a bowl of water and place a quarter on top of it. Return it to the freezer*
- ❏ Thermostat adjusted appropriately?
- ❏ Unplugged computers, TVs, treadmills or other exercise equipment?
- ❏ Windows closed and locked?
- ❏ Blinds/curtains pulled?
- ❏ Light and/or radio in a front room on a timer?
- ❏ Home alarm set?
- ❏ Doors locked?

*If you lose electricity while you're gone, the water will thaw and the quarter will drop. You'll know that you need to deal with your food appropriately.

My Water Storage Plan

I have _____ people in my family.

Using the rule of one gallon per person per day…

I need _____ gallons of water for my family to live for three days.

I need _____ gallons of water for my family to live a week.

I need _____ gallons of water for my family to live a month.

In order to get to my needed amount of water (whether it's three days, one week, or one month) I plan to store . . .

_____ cases of water (approximately three gallons per case)

_____ water bricks (three gallons per water brick)

_____ five-gallon camping water containers

_____ fifty-five-gallon barrels

_____ WaterBobs

When the water runs out….

State laws dealing with rainwater catchment can be found here:
http://www.ncsl.org/research/environment-and-natural-resources/rainwater-harvesting.aspx#State
My rainwater catchment law(s) says that I (circle one) can / can with restrictions / cannot catch rainwater.

My restrictions are:

_____

_____

_____

Rainwater catchment, if you are allowed to by your state's laws, should always be your first backup for your stored water.

I have a Pinterest board set up specifically to deal with water storage and rainwater catchment. There are a bunch of plans for building your own rainwater catchment systems there. You can find it here: https://www.pinterest.com/AYearWithoutTheGroceryStore/water-water-everywhere/

The rainwater catchment system that I decided on is:

_____

Congratulations on working your way through this workbook. Feeling a bit more prepared? Or at least having a more of an idea a direction for getting prepared. I hope the Facebook group has been an encouragement as well.

Preparedness is so incredibly multi-faceted, and food storage is just *one* of the facets. It is, however, one of the most important facets of taking care of your family in an emergency. Having this aspect in place is the perfect springboard to getting other areas of family preparedness in order.

You've already taken the first step, and that's the hardest one. Keep taking steps. Continue to interact in the Facebook group. Continue to learn more about the aspects of preparedness that you've really enjoyed. If there are aspects of preparedness that you know you are weak in , figure out how to shore them up. Join other preparedness groups, too and get their take on things too. Forge friendships. Find new constructive hobbies. Enjoy your journey to preparedness. I'm glad to have you along as part of mine.

So after working through the workbook, how long can YOU go without the grocery store?

Printed in Great Britain
by Amazon